How To Trade For A Living

A Beginner's Guide to Navigating Financial Markets, Building Wealth, and Achieving Trading Success

By

Dick P. Blair

Contents

Introduction

Understanding financial markets

Assets such as shares, indices, currencies, commodities, and more can be bought and sold in financial markets by both individuals and businesses.

Financial markets have been traded for hundreds of years. They were born out of a practical requirement to facilitate faster money raising for businesses in need of it and to enable consumers purchase and sell goods more effectively.

Markets have expanded in size and speed over time, and more individuals than ever before have access to them. They used to be exclusive to very affluent people, financial houses, and large banks. However, it is no longer the case.

Financial markets are divided into asset classes because they are so diverse. Here is a summary of a few that you may come upon.

Currency

Forex markets, sometimes referred to as FX, are where global currencies, including the US dollar, the euro, and the British pound, are bought and sold 24 hours a day.

Commodities

Commodities are tangible goods that are utilized or consumed by humans, other animals, or businesses. Among the notable examples are oil, silver, and gold.

Stocks

Also referred to as shares or equities. Investing in a certain firm that is listed on a stock market is what stock trading is all about. Well-known instances include Microsoft, BP, and Apple.

Indices

A set of shares' prices are tracked by an index. One of the most traded indexes in the world, the S&P 500 (US 500), for instance, measures some of the biggest US listed firms.

Fixed Earnings

Any asset that gives its owner a fixed, recurring interest payment is considered fixed income. Bonds are the most popular example, although there are many more kinds of fixed income instruments.

Digital Money

The 'newest' category of assets available. Cryptocurrencies are money that have no central bank backing and are instead supported by cryptography. Bitcoin is the most well-known cryptocurrency and the original one.

What has an impact on the markets?

Although every asset has specific elements that influence its price, supply and demand—a basic law of economics—are the primary forces behind market prices.

Supply

The amount of a financial market that is accessible for purchase is known as supply. When there is a high demand for a product but a limited supply, the price will increase. Then, if supply increases without demand increasing, the price will often decrease.

Demand

Demand is the number of individuals attempting to purchase a financial market. A market's price will decrease if supply is greater than demand.

The price of that item will often increase if demand increases but supply does not.

A financial asset's supply might change for a variety of reasons. If a central bank were to decide to raise the money supply, for instance, the price of currency would decline since there would be a lot more of it accessible. On the other hand, the supply of gold is reliant on several businesses, organizations, and nations worldwide.

A few key elements to be aware of when it comes to demand are as follows:

- News: A lot of market players monitor the news in real time; favorable or unfavorable headlines can swiftly reduce supply or demand.
- Policy of the central bank: Decisions made by central banks, such as adjustments to interest rates, may have a big impact on how money moves across the globe and will definitely affect demand.
- Official Data Demand: may be impacted by official releases. Data on inflation and unemployment, for instance, provide insight into the health of an economy and may attract investors.

Data analysis and market trends

The contemporary oracle, revealing secrets about obscure markets and hidden trends. When used properly, it may be a powerful tool that clears the murky seas of finance and points traders in the direction of lucrative opportunities. But worry not—with the correct resources and a dash of bravery, even the most inexperienced skipper can learn to manage the waves of data.

Dive into the Depths:

- Cast your Net: Identify relevant data sources – market statistics, news feeds, social media sentiment, even satellite imagery! The wider your net, the more comprehensive your picture of the market's tides.
- Eliminate the Catch: Not all information is made equal. Eliminate irregularities, noise, and inconsistent data. It is clear information that feeds your analysis, not muddled data.
- See the Treasure: Your treasure maps may be made from graphs, charts, and even heatmaps. To uncover the underlying currents that are concealed, visualize trends, correlations, and patterns.

How to Read the Whispers:

- Correlation, not Causation: Trends aren't guarantees, just hints from the market's oracle. Don't mistake correlation for causation – a rising tide might lift all boats, but not every rising tide leads to riches.

- Context is Everything: Just like a single word, data requires context to be fully understood. Before making any judgments, take into account market mood, industry news, and economic variables.
- The Story Is Important Because: Data points are parts of a bigger story. Combine them to create a narrative that clarifies the "why" behind the "what." A good story is more valuable than a thousand spreadsheets.

Remember:

- Utilize data as a tool, not a crystal ball, and let it guide rather than dictate your choices. Throughout your trading career, risk management, experience, and intuition will all be very important.
- Beware of Overfitting: Avoid overfitting by not forcing data to match your assumptions. Keep an eye out for unforeseen currents and modify your route as necessary.

- Continue Learning and Adapting: The market is an ever-changing environment. To stay ahead of the curve, always improve your data analysis abilities, investigate new resources, and maintain your flexibility.

Bonus Tip: Stay afloat in the data sea! Concentrate on a few essential variables that are pertinent to your trading objectives and technique. Less is more in certain situations, particularly when there is an abundance of information.

Thus, embrace the potential of data analysis, but keep in mind that it's a tool, not a road plan. You may successfully navigate the data-driven currents of the market and find your own profitable jewels if you have a healthy dose of skepticism, critical thinking, and a voracious appetite for information.

Keyword research in trading

Doing trade keyword research! Sifting through mountains of verbiage to find the bright nuggets of insight that may propel your marketing to prosperity is like digging for gold. But have no fear, I'm here to arm you with your pick and pan so you can hit it rich in the keyword jungle.

Make a map of your territory first:

- Recognize your audience: Who are you attempting to draw in? Are you a swing trader, day trader, or long-term investor? Selecting the appropriate keywords requires an understanding of their language and demands.
- Identify your niche: Are you promoting a cutting-edge new trading platform, instructional materials, or tools for technical analysis? Knowing your unique selling proposition helps narrow down your keyword hunting ground.
- Spy on the competition: See what keywords your rivals are using. Analyze their websites, social media,

and online ads to uncover hidden treasures you might have missed.

Let's now search for those ideal keywords:

- Go to the keyword mines: Ahrefs, Semrush, and Google Keyword Planner. These are your go-to sieves and shovels for sifting through data and finding hidden gems.
- Think like a trader: Think like a trader and come up with a list of possible search phrases for your target market. Employ industry lingo, widely used acronyms, and even trading axioms to expand your reach.
- Tailor your search: Don't just focus on broad keywords like "trading." Get specific! "Day trading strategies for volatile markets" is a much more valuable nugget than just "trading."

Refine your haul:

- Analyze search volume: Examine search volume and select keywords that will provide enough traffic to your page without overwhelming your readers with too much competition. Just fine! Think of Goldilocks and the phrase porridge!

- Think about the competition: Are you really a genuine contender for those high-volume beauties? Smaller, more specialized keywords might occasionally be more profitable conversions and are also simpler to dominate.

- Think long-term: Plan ahead and don't follow the latest fads. Select keywords that have longevity, meaning they won't become outdated like yesterday's news. Not fads in the market, but long-term, solid gold bullion are what you want in keywords.

Remember that:

- It is not appropriate to overuse keywords in your text like a magpie collecting sparkling objects. Keywords are tools, not objectives. Make smart use of them to draw in the correct audience and provide real value.

- Remain adaptable: Just as markets change, so do keywords. To make sure your treasure map is current, keep doing research, keeping an eye out for trends, and modifying your approach.
- Try and improve: Don't be scared to test out various keywords and monitor their effectiveness. Determine what appeals to your audience and modify your strategy accordingly.

Bonus Tip: Experiment with other search engines! Look through industry magazines, social media groups, and forums that are pertinent to your target audience to find out what language they use naturally.

So venture out, daring business owner! Equipped with your expertise in keyword research and a voracious appetite for information, you may successfully negotiate the perilous landscape of internet marketing and win over the hearts and minds of your target trading audience. I hope your keywords shine brightly and take you to a place where leads flow freely and conversions thrive!

Remember that conducting keyword research is a never-ending journey, a never-ending search for undiscovered gems. Accept the excitement of the pursuit, relish the process of learning, and see how your online presence draws in the traders you are looking for.

Chapter 1

Analyzing successful trading books

Book exchanges! Mounds of paper containing proverbs, battle tales, and the odd recipe for ruining your finances. But brave merchant, where do you even begin? How do you go through the pile of pages to find the pearls of wisdom that will help you become an expert in your market? Do not be worried; I am here to help you navigate the maze-like archives of trading expertise!

Choosing Your Path:

- Know your goals: Are you looking for a practical manual for a certain trading strategy, a philosophical approach to the market, or insights into technical analysis? Choosing the correct map (or book) is aided by knowing where you're going.

- Explore a variety of environments; don't limit yourself to one genre. Step outside your comfort zone and investigate trading psychology, risk management, and fundamental analysis. Every book adds a different viewpoint to your adventure.
- Look for the legends: Get up on the backs of the giants! Pick up a book by Jesse Livermore, Peter Lynch, or Jack Schwager. Their timeless wisdom, though born in different market eras, still holds valuable lessons for modern traders.

Breaking the Code:

- Refrain from taking the hook completely: Every book, just like any trade, demands critical thought. Examine the author's biases, refute their presumptions, and put their methods to the test using your own findings and experiences.
- Make the connection: Don't think of a book as a standalone work. Look for the connections between them, the recurring themes that appear in various trading philosophies. It is from this combination that genuine understanding arises.

- Sharpen your tools: Make your tools sharp by using the book as a whetstone for your critical thinking abilities. Acquire proficiency with novel technical indicators, enhance your risk mitigation strategies, and broaden your comprehension of market psychology. You should get crisper and more organized with each page.

Remember:

- Your best instructor will always be experience; no book can ever fully replace the lessons you'll acquire in the actual market. Make use of the information you've read to launch your own research and exploration.
- Trade with your heart, but control your head: Feelings are natural parts of the game, but keep them from impairing your judgment. To maintain mental clarity and make disciplined judgments, apply the lessons learned from books on trading psychology.
- The trip holds the true value: avoid skimming the pages in a frenzied attempt to get answers. Savor

the educational process, the intellectual challenge, and the gradual growth that comes with each insightful chapter.

Bonus Tip: Never undervalue the influence of a community! Talk about your insights with other traders in person or virtually. By exchanging ideas and experiences, you can make each book even more valuable and advance your group's trading knowledge.

So, dear merchant! Explore the vast world of trade books, but never forget that information is useless without use. Make your own way to financial independence by refining your tactics, controlling your risks, and applying the principles you've learned from these books. I hope your reading lamp serves as your road map to market mastery and your bookcase as your hidden treasure!

Remember that the real worth of a trading book is found not only in its words but also in the way it piques your interest, sharpens your analytical skills, and helps you advance into being a more knowledgeable and competent trader.

Strengths and Weaknesses of Existing Books

The modest trading tome! Those paper oracles that whisper wealth and market dominance secrets. However, just like any treasure map, their direction isn't perfect. So, daring trader, let's put on our reading glasses and set out on a careful investigation to determine the advantages and disadvantages of these market bibles.

Strengths to Savor

- Foundational Frameworks: Any prospective trader should start with classic literature like "Trading in the Zone" by Mark Douglas or "Technical Analysis of the Financial Markets" by John Murphy. They provide technological tools, enduring concepts, and a firm grasp of market dynamics.
- Different Viewpoints: There are a plethora of trading philosophies! Each book illuminates a distinct

trading style, enhancing your comprehension of the market environment. Examples of these styles include the aggressive trend-following of Richard Dennis and the stoic risk management of Ed Seykota.

- Real-World Relatable: Some publications, such as "Market Wizards" by Jack Schwager, tell the stories of prosperous traders and their ups and downs. These stories offer invaluable insights into the emotional roller coaster of trading, reminding us that we're not alone in this financial jungle.

Things to Watch Out For

- Outdated tactics: Because markets change quickly, much like chameleons, some older publications may contain tactics that are out of current for the fast-paced, algorithmic trading environment of today. Be careful what you wish!
- Oversimplified Solutions: Books that promise "get rich quick" schemes or assert to have cracked the market code should be avoided. Success in trading is rarely the result of magic beans; instead, it's a

marathon powered by perseverance and never-ending education.

- Biased Points of View: Each writer has their own set of prejudices and trade wounds. Don't take anything they say at face value. Examine their reasoning critically, try out their tactics on practice accounts, and develop your own unique trading philosophy.

Remember that:

- No Book Is a Holy Grail: View trading books as helpful resources rather than final solutions. The market is a beast that never stops learning, and so should you.
- It's Important to Use Critical Thinking: Don't read through every page. Examine, evaluate, and refute the author's presumptions. The most useful instrument you have in this intellectual treasure hunt is your own critical thinking.
- Experience is the Ultimate Teacher: no book can ever fully replace the knowledge gained from working in the actual market. Make use of the

information you've read to launch your own research and exploration.

Bonus Tip: Diversify your literary diet! Don't get stuck in one genre or author. Examine various trading strategies, psychological perspectives, and even historical research to have a comprehensive grasp of the market and your position in it.

So, daring merchant! Make your way through the maze of trade literature with an insatiable curiosity and a critical eye. It's important to keep in mind that a book's real worth comes from how it challenges you as a reader, sharpens your analytical skills, and helps you become a more knowledgeable and competent trader.

Chapter 2

Seeking guidance from industry professional

It is undoubtedly a good idea to consult with industry experts, particularly in a complicated area like trading. Here's a tip on how to go about asking experts in the trading sector for advice:

1. Identify Your Objectives: Make sure that your trading goals and objectives are clearly stated. Are you seeking guidance on certain markets, trading tactics, risk control, or advancing your career in the trading sector?
2. Research and Networking: Participate in networking events, conferences, and seminars for the sector. Meeting experts, getting to know their experiences, and maybe making connections are all made possible by this.
3. Virtual Channels: Participate in trading-related social media groups, online forums, and communities. In

these forums, a lot of seasoned experts exchange knowledge and counsel.

4. Professional groups: Consider becoming a member of organizations or professional groups pertaining to trading. These organizations frequently offer platforms for networking with seasoned professionals or mentorship programs.

5. Reach Out Respectfully: Find experts whose background fits your objectives. Use email or other professional ways to politely get in touch with them. Make your intentions clear and ask for their advice.

6. Informative Interviews: Ask experts in the trade sector to do informative interviews. Prepare intelligent queries regarding their professional trajectories, obstacles they overcame, and lessons discovered.

7. Attend Workshops and Webinars: Take part in training sessions, webinars, and workshops led by specialists in the field. This gives you the opportunity to speak with them personally and obtain useful knowledge at the same time.

8. Use mentoring Programs: A few trade companies and colleges provide mentoring programs. Take advantage

of these chances to find a mentor who can help you by sharing their expertise.

9. Continuous Learning: Show that you are dedicated to lifelong learning by keeping up with market trends, industry trends, and trade tactics. Professionals are more inclined to interact with people who genuinely care about them and are committed.

10. Build a Professional Online Presence: Make use of websites like LinkedIn to establish a polished online presence. To project oneself as a serious and dedicated trader, participate in conversations, share your analysis, and provide your opinions.

11. Show Gratitude and Respect: Express thanks to experts who take the time to provide advice. Consider building a long-term professional connection instead of requesting one-time counsel, and show them respect for their time.

Though the trading sector can be very competitive, experts frequently value zeal and a sincere desire to learn. Be humble in your interactions, open to learning, and genuinely motivated to advance in your career.

Gaining Insights into Effective Approaches

Gaining knowledge about practical strategies
Understanding successful trading strategies requires a
combination of learning from seasoned experts, keeping
up with market developments, and persistent self-
improvement. Here is a list of practical strategies for
traders:

1. Trading Strategies, Education, and Skill Development:
   Ongoing Education: Remain current with market
   movements, financial news, and trading tactics. To
   expand your expertise, read credible books, take part
   in webinars, and attend seminars.
   - Fundamental and Technical Analysis: Gain
     proficiency in both fundamental and technical
     analysis. Recognize how market movements, chart
     patterns, and economic factors affect trading
     choices.
2. Measurement of Risk; Set a Clear Risk Tolerance:
   Specify the level of risk you are willing to take on and
   create a plan for managing it. To guard against large

losses, only risk a tiny portion of your trading money on any one deal.

- Make use of stop-loss orders. Use stop-loss orders to reduce possible losses by automatically exiting a transaction when it hits a predefined threshold.

3. Plan for Trading: Make a thorough trading strategy: Create a thorough trading strategy that details your objectives, approaches, guidelines for managing risk, and standards for entering and leaving transactions.

- Follow Your Plan: It's important to maintain discipline. Follow your trading strategy and refrain from acting rashly in response to transient market swings or emotional states.

4. Market Analysis: Recognize Market Conditions: Examine the market environment and modify your plans as necessary. Recognize the difference between range and trending markets and modify your strategy accordingly.

- Apply a Variety of Analysis Methods: To make educated trading decisions, combine technical, fundamental, and sentiment analysis.

5. Ongoing Assessment and Adjustment: Examine and Assess Trades: Consistently examine your transactions, whether profitable or not, to spot trends and opportunities for development.
    - Adjust to Modifying Market Circumstances: As markets change, so do successful traders. Remain adaptable and modify your tactics to conform to evolving market circumstances.
6. Emotional Self-Control: Effectively Handle Emotions: Having emotional control is essential while trading. Don't let fear or greed influence your judgments. Remain composed and reasonable while you're winning or losing.
    - Take Rest Periods When Required: Take a pause if you notice yourself becoming too worked up or upset. Before making any significant trading choices, clear your head.
7. Collaboration and Networking: Establish Connections with Other Traders: Talk to other traders in person and virtually. Talk about tactics, exchange thoughts, and gain knowledge from other traders' experiences.
    - Think About Mentoring: Consult mentors or seasoned traders for advice. Getting knowledge

from the experiences of others might yield insightful information and success shortcuts.

8. Make Use of Technology: Keep Up with Trading Platform Updates: Get acquainted with cutting-edge trading platforms and resources. Algorithmic trading and automation can improve productivity.

   - Applying Analytical Instruments: To improve your decision-making, make use of computational models, charting software, and technical analysis tools.

9. Assess and Control Expenses: Reduce Transaction charges: Mind the spreads, fees, and transaction charges. These may have an effect on your total earnings.

   - Assess Tax Repercussions: Recognize the tax ramifications of your trading activity and plan to reduce your tax obligations.

10. Monitor Performance and Objectives: Maintain Comprehensive Records: Keep a thorough record of all of your transactions, including entry and exit points, justifications, and results. Performance analysis benefits from this.

- Review and Adjust Goals: Regularly assess your trading objectives and make necessary adjustments in light of your developing abilities, level of risk tolerance, and state of the market.

You may improve your ability to make decisions, control risks, and strive for steady success in the fast-paced world of trading by implementing these practical strategies into your trading career. Recall that learning new things in trading is a lifelong process, and that flexibility is essential for sustained success.

Chapter 3

Risk Management in Trading

Risk management isn't about wearing metaphorical bubble wrap (unless you're trading options on antique porcelain, then maybe). It's about taking control. It's about building a fortress around your precious capital, a fortress with walls of discipline, moats of knowledge, and gates guarded by stop-losses and take-profits.

Think of your trading journey as a high-wire act. Every trade is a tightrope walk across a canyon of uncertainty. But before you even step onto the wire, you need a safety net. That net is your risk management plan. It's your pre-flight checklist, your map through the fog, your "don't walk blindfolded into a tornado" guide.

So, what goes into this magical risk management plan?

- Know your limits: Be honest with yourself. How much can you afford to lose on a single trade? Don't be a cowboy throwing your entire ranch on a single card draw. Set a risk percentage based on your account size and emotional fortitude.

- Befriend stop-losses: These are your automatic brakes, your "get me out of here!" button when the market turns south faster than a penguin on ice. Use them wisely, but use them.

- Don't chase waterfalls: Greed is a seductive siren song, luring you towards ever-increasing positions and potential riches. But remember, the higher the potential reward, the higher the risk. Stick to your plan, your pre-determined risk and position size.

- Diversify your portfolio: Don't put all your eggs in one basket (or all your bitcoin in one exchange). Spread your bets across different assets, markets, and strategies. This way, if one basket falls, the others can cushion the blow.

- Embrace the knowledge: Risk management isn't just about rules and numbers. It's about understanding the market, the technical and fundamental factors that make it tick. This knowledge gives you the power to anticipate risks and adjust your sails accordingly.

Remember, risk management isn't about eliminating risk. It's about managing it. It's about accepting that the market is a wild beast, and you, my friend, are the tamer. With the right tools and mindset, you can turn that risky business into a thriving venture, a testament to your skill and discipline in the face of the financial jungle.
So, go forth, trader! Embrace the dance, manage the dragon, and remember a well-planned risk is a calculated win.

Bonus tip: Don't forget to reward yourself for smart risk management. Every time you stick to your plan and avoid a potential disaster, celebrate! A small victory dance, a fancy coffee treat – you deserve it!

Developing Strategies for Risk Mitigation

Risk mitigation! It's like playing chess with fate, strategically placing your pawns of precaution to outmaneuver the dangers lurking on the board. But instead of a dusty old game room, the battlefield here is the vast, dynamic landscape of life itself. Whether you're tackling a business venture, navigating personal finances, or even planning your next vacation, crafting effective risk mitigation strategies is the ultimate armor against uncertainty.

So, where do we begin? Let's crack open the toolbox and explore some potent tools:

- The Foresight Gambit: Don't be a sheep charging blindly into the herd. Channel your inner fortune teller (minus the crystal ball, thank goodness) and identify potential risks. What could go wrong? From market upheavals to unexpected setbacks, map out the possible pitfalls. Think like a seasoned warrior anticipating enemy maneuvers.

- The Diversification Defense: Remember the fable of the eggs and the basket? Don't put all your hopes (and finances) in one fragile container. Spread your bets, diversify your investments, and explore different avenues. This way, if one leg of your stool wobbles, you still have others to keep you upright.

- The Contingency Counterattack: Don't be caught flat-footed when the storm hits. Prepare contingency plans like a chess grandmaster with backup strategies. Have an emergency fund for financial mishaps, a backup plan for project snags, and a rain-or-shine alternative for your outdoor adventure. Be the one with multiple umbrellas in your backpack, ready for any downpour.
- The Knowledge Arsenal: Information is power, especially when it comes to mitigating risks. Stay informed, research potential threats, and learn from the experiences of others. Read up on investment strategies, attend risk management workshops, and don't be afraid to ask for expert advice. Remember, knowledge is your shield against the unknown.
- The Adaptability Agility: The world is a shifting dance floor, and you need to be the most nimble dancer on it. Be flexible and adaptable. Adjust your strategies as needed, pivot when circumstances change, and don't be afraid to abandon a sinking ship. Remember, sometimes the best risk mitigation is admitting course correction is necessary.

- The Monitoring Mantra: Don't set your plan and forget it. Constantly monitor and assess the situation. Be vigilant, like a hawk scanning the horizon. Track your progress, identify emerging risks, and adjust your defenses accordingly. This proactive approach keeps you one step ahead of the ever-changing game.

Bonus Tip: Don't let fear paralyze you. A healthy dose of caution is wise, but don't let it turn into debilitating anxiety. Embrace calculated risks; they can often lead to the greatest rewards. Just remember, even the most skilled chess player takes calculated risks to win the game. Developing effective risk mitigation strategies is an ongoing process, an ever-evolving dance with uncertainty. But by equipping yourself with the right tools and mindset, you can transform uncertainty into opportunity, navigate the challenges of life with confidence, and ultimately emerge victorious from the game of fate.

So, May your foresight be sharp, your defenses strong, and your adaptability legendary! And remember, even the occasional pawn sacrifice can lead to a thrilling checkmate.

Chapter 4

Technical Analysis in Trading

Technical analysis is the secret deciphering ring for market riddles, the language of charts and whispers of indicators. To some, it's a mysterious dance of Fibonacci spirals and moving averages. To others, it's a powerful tool in their financial toolbox, a compass that helps them navigate the turbulent waters of the market. Nevertheless, worry not—both novice navigators and seasoned captains will find this to be a straightforward tutorial to the interesting field of technical analysis.

To begin with, visualize the market as a huge ocean. Trends ripple like currents, prices rise and fall like tides, and volatility storms can form out of nowhere. As your sextant, technical analysis will help you navigate your path, anticipate these swells and currents, and steer clear of dangerous reefs.

What tools are in our treasure box of charts then?

- Candlesticks: These vibrant tiny warriors narrate stories about fights in the market. Their wicks and shadows tell of bearish retreats and bullish successes. When you can understand their language, the murmurs in the market will soon become roars.

- Moving averages: These slick lines, which represent the overall tendency of the ocean, are comparable to dependable old sea dogs. They assist you in determining the general direction of the stream and helping you see through the turbulent waves.

- Indicators: These high-tech devices blink and emit beeps to expose secrets under the surface. Each indicator provides a different viewpoint on the hidden depths of the market, from the Bollinger Bands signaling volatility to the Relative Strength Index measuring market momentum.

However, keep in mind that technical analysis isn't a magic orb. Yes, it's a strong tool, but it's not a miraculous potion that will bring wealth. Make sensible use of it by combining technology with basic analysis and a good dose of common sense.

The following are some golden guidelines to remember:

- Don't chase rainbows: Don't follow every chart pattern or indication signal at face value. Exercise critical thinking, consider the wider picture, and keep in mind that previous achievement does not guarantee future outcomes.
- Verification is crucial: Never depend just on one indicator. Before making a fresh trade, seek confirmation from other tools and technical signs.
- Adjust and change: The market is a dynamic animal that is always shifting its preferences. If the technical analysis no longer presents a compelling picture, be adaptable, change your tactics, and don't be afraid to bail on a failing venture.

Note that technical analysis is not a science, but rather an art. It all comes down to reading the market's signals, comprehending its language, and applying that information to make wise choices. Thus, take your compass and map, go out with a cautious optimism, and sail the market's ocean with the knowledge of an experienced captain and the shrewdness of a pirate. And who knows—you could find success in the unexplored field of technical analysis!

Bonus Advice: Remember to have fun! With its many obstacles and surprising discoveries, the market can be an exhilarating journey. Savor the process of picking up new skills, trying out ideas, and becoming an expert in technical analysis. Even the most experienced captain had to start somewhere, after all.

Applying Technical Analysis for Decision Making

Technical analysis, with its alluring vocabulary of moving averages, moving average correlation coefficients, and Fibonacci spirals, entices traders with the prospect of penetrating the dark corners of the market and discovering undiscovered wealth. However, let's first negotiate the challenging terrain of using technical analysis for decision-making before plunging headfirst into a sea of data.

Recall that technical analysis is not a crystal ball that flashes unchanging facts. It functions more like a reliable map, providing insightful information without promising a treasure trove at each indicated X.

So, how can we make use of this map without becoming bogged down in a maze of shapes and lines?

- Accept the Compass Instead of the Crown: Consider technical analysis as a compass that points you in the right direction without telling you where to go. To find possible trading chances, use indicators like as trendlines and moving averages, but don't just follow them at random. Recall that the market is a fickle creature, and that unforeseen storms may derail even the most accurate compass.
- Seek Confirmation Rather Than Certainty: Don't take any one sign at face value. Seek convergence, on the other hand, when several technical indications converge in the same direction.

Envision comparing your map to the sun, stars, and even the murmurs of experienced sailors. Your level of confidence in your trading judgments increases with the amount of confirmation you have.

- Never forget that context is essential: Technical analysis is not sufficient on its own. Think about the wider picture, which includes important elements like world events, business trends, and economic news. In the face of an imminent recession, even the most flawless chart pattern can be meaningless. Thus, keep an eye on the wider market and use it to guide how you read technical indications.

- Be a Strategist, Not a Gambler: You shouldn't use technical analysis as a justification for rash trading decisions. Create a clear trading plan that includes criteria for risk management, entry and exit points, and position sizing recommendations. Instead of replacing your plan with a chart dice toss, use technical analysis to improve it.

- Learn, Adapt and Evolve: The market is a dynamic kaleidoscope that is always changing. What was effective yesterday may not be so tomorrow. Remain modest, continue to pick up new technical skills and tactics, and modify your plan in response to changing market conditions. Recall that the finest traders are not those who stick to antiquated charts, but rather those who can manage the constantly shifting currents.

Chapter 5

Developing a Trading Plan

The humble trading plan – the unsung hero of financial ventures. Often relegated to dusty notebooks and forgotten spreadsheets, it holds the key to navigating the turbulent waters of the market with grace and purpose.

Let's shed light on this often-overlooked treasure map and transform it into your secret weapon for trading success.

1. Crafting Your Compass: Think of your trading plan as a personalized GPS for the financial jungle. It charts your course, sets your boundaries, and helps you avoid getting lost in the wilderness of impulsive decisions. But unlike your average GPS, this one requires your active participation. Here's how to build your own:

   - Know Yourself: Before charting your path, understand your risk tolerance, preferred trading style (day trader, swing trader, etc.), and available capital. Are you a cautious explorer or a thrill-seeking adventurer? Knowing your comfort zone is crucial for setting realistic goals and managing expectations.

2. Define Your Destination: Where do you see yourself in the market? Short-term gains or long-term wealth building? Setting clear and achievable goals gives your journey direction and purpose. Remember, even the mightiest galleon needs a clear destination to avoid aimlessly drifting at sea.

3. Chart Your Course: Identify your trading strategies, risk management parameters, and entry and exit points for trades. Think of these as your navigational tools, helping you make informed decisions in the heat of the moment. Don't jump on a ship without knowing your port of call!

4. Weather the Storms: No journey is smooth sailing. Prepare for market volatility and unexpected setbacks by setting stop-loss orders and defining your risk per trade. Remember, even the most skilled captain encounters choppy waters, but a good plan ensures you weather the storm with minimal damage.

5. Adapt and Evolve: The market is a living beast, constantly changing its tune. Be flexible enough to adjust your plan based on new information and changing market conditions. Think of it as updating your nautical charts with newly discovered reefs and shifting currents.

Remember:

- Consistency is Key: Sticking to your plan is like following a reliable star chart. It builds discipline, fosters trust in your own decisions, and keeps you from sailing off course on impulses.
- Don't Fear Revisions: Your trading plan isn't set in stone. As you gain experience and the market evolves, don't hesitate to revisit and refine your strategies. Think of it as fine-tuning your instruments for a more accurate journey.
- Celebrate the Journey: Remember, the pursuit of financial freedom is an adventure, not a race. Enjoy the process of learning, adapting, and mastering the art of trading. Every market fluctuation is a valuable

lesson, every closed trade a step closer to your destination.

So, Dear trader! With a well-crafted and meticulously adhered-to trading plan, you'll navigate the market with confidence, resilience, and a clear vision of your financial goals. May your journey be profitable, your decisions inspired, and your course charted with wisdom and precision.

Response to Setting Trading Goals

Trading goals, like kites in a financial hurricane, can be easily swept away by ambition or deflated by fear. But fret not, intrepid trader, for with the right approach, your goals can become sturdy anchors, guiding you towards a prosperous voyage. Let's explore the art of crafting trading goals that are SMART and SIZZLING:

- S is for Specific: Vagueness is the enemy of progress. Ditch the "get rich quick" dreams and define your goals with laser focus. Do you want to achieve a specific percentage return? Increase your account size by a certain amount? Mastering a new trading strategy? The more specific, the more likely you are to chart a clear path and celebrate your victories along the way.

- M is for Measurable: How will you know you've reached your destination? Numbers are the compass points on your financial map. Set quantifiable goals – a target profit figure, a desired number of successful trades, or even a specific level of technical analysis mastery. Measurable goals keep you accountable and fueled by tangible progress.
- A is for Attainable: Don't set yourself up for disappointment by aiming for the moon on your first lunar landing. Start with realistic goals based on your current skill level, market conditions, and available capital. Gradually increase the difficulty as you gain experience and confidence. Remember, even Everest was once just a hill for ambitious mountaineers.
- R is for Relevant: Align your goals with your overall trading vision. Do they support your long-term financial objectives? Are they compatible with your

risk tolerance and preferred trading style? Don't chase someone else's gold; mine your own unique path to financial freedom.

- T is for Time-Bound: Give your goals a deadline! Setting a timeframe adds urgency and focus. Aim for short-term milestones that ladder up to your long-term aspirations. Celebrate smaller wins along the way, keeping the spark of motivation alive.

Now, let's add some Sizzle:

- Make them Dreamworthy: Don't just set goals, set your soul on fire with them! Visualize the things your success will unlock — the financial freedom, the sense of accomplishment, the ability to pursue your passions. Emotionally charged goals keep you inspired and resilient in the face of market challenges.
- Break them Down: Large goals can feel overwhelming. Chunk them down into smaller, actionable steps. Celebrate mastering a new technical indicator, achieving a successful trade

streak, or completing a financial book – each step paves the way for the grand finale.

- Reward Yourself: Don't treat every goal as a grueling marathon. Schedule mini-celebrations for reaching milestones. A fancy coffee, a weekend getaway, or even a simple pat on the back – acknowledge your progress and keep the excitement bubbling.

Remember, trading goals are more than just numbers on a page. They are the roadmap to your financial dreams, the wind in your sails, the fuel for your trading engine. Set them with precision, ignite them with passion, and watch them propel you towards a prosperous and fulfilling trading journey!

So, go forth, ambitious trader, and let your goals reach for the sky! May your journey be fruitful, your targets met, and your financial dreams take flight.

Creating a Trading Strategy

The trading strategy – the elusive Holy Grail of the market, the secret sauce that separates winners from well-wishers. Fear not, intrepid trader, for today we embark on a quest to forge your own personalized weapon for financial conquest. But remember, strategy isn't a magic spell; it's a map, a compass, a guiding light in the often-turbulent ocean of the market.

- Know Yourself: Before charting your course, understand your risk tolerance, preferred trading style (day trader, swing trader, etc.), and available capital. Are you a cautious turtle or a daring shark? Knowing your comfort zone is crucial for choosing the right tools and tailoring your strategy.
- Define Your Destination: Where do you see yourself in the market? Short-term profits or long-term wealth building? Setting clear and achievable goals gives your strategy purpose and direction. Remember, even the mightiest galleon needs a clear destination to avoid aimlessly drifting at sea.

- Choose Your Arsenal: The market offers a dazzling array of tools: technical analysis, fundamental analysis, news events, market psychology – the list goes on. Identify the tools that resonate with your style and build your strategy around them. Don't try to juggle too many apples – focus on mastering a few that give you a clear edge.
- Sharpen Your Sword: Technical analysis offers a treasure trove of indicators and patterns, but remember, they're not crystal balls. Learn to interpret them with caution, seek confirmation from multiple sources, and never blindly follow their every whisper. Hone your skills, test on demo accounts, and become a master of your analytical tools.
- Build Your Fortress: Risk management is your impenetrable shield. Define your risk per trade, set stop-loss orders diligently, and stick to your limits like a warrior to their oath. Remember, even the bravest knight needs strong defenses to survive the battlefield.
- Adapt and Evolve: The market is a living beast, constantly changing its tune. Be flexible enough to adjust your strategy based on new information and

changing market conditions. Think of it as updating your nautical charts with newly discovered reefs and shifting currents.

- Test and Refine: Your strategy isn't set in stone. Backtest it on historical data, fine-tune it based on real-time experience, and don't be afraid to throw out what doesn't work. Remember, even the most skilled sculptor chisels away at the stone until they reveal the masterpiece within.
- Be Patient and Persistent: Rome wasn't built in a day, and fortunes aren't amassed overnight. Be patient with your strategy, give it time to unfold, and trust in the process. Persistence and discipline are the keys to unlocking the market's secrets.

Bonus Tip: Don't let emotions cloud your judgment. Fear and greed are the market's siren song, luring traders to shipwreck. Stick to your strategy, prioritize discipline over emotions, and celebrate the journey, not just the destination.

So, intrepid trader! With a well-crafted and rigorously tested strategy, you'll navigate the market with confidence, resilience, and a clear vision of your financial goals. May your journey be profitable, your decisions precise, and your market compass always point you towards success. Bon voyage!

Remember, the market is a journey, not a race. Enjoy the thrill of the hunt, the satisfaction of a well-executed trade, and the freedom that financial success can bring. And above all, never lose sight of the adventure – for that's the true treasure buried within the heart of every trader.

Implementing and Adjusting the Trading Plan

The trading plan – that valiant roadmap to financial freedom, sometimes crumpled in sweaty pockets, other times proudly displayed on the trading altar. Implementing and adjusting it can feel like sailing a stormy sea, filled with both exhilarating swells and terrifying crashes. But fear not, for with the right approach, your plan can become your trusty anchor, guiding you through turbulent markets and towards your financial goals.

Setting Sail:

- Unfurl the Parchment: Dust off your plan, reread its every line, and remind yourself of your destination. Visualize your goals, feel the excitement of reaching them, and let that ignite your commitment to the course.
- Calibrate the Compass: Check if your risk tolerance or preferred style has evolved. Have new tools like indicators or strategies caught your eye? Update your plan to reflect your current trading persona.
- Provision for the Journey: Ensure your capital, risk parameters, and entry/exit points are still aligned with your goals and market realities. A plan needs adaptable supplies, not outdated rations.

Navigating the Currents:

- Chart the Winds: Monitor market conditions, economic news, and industry trends. Adjust your course slightly, but don't abandon ship at every gust. Remember, flexibility doesn't mean constant chaos.

- Heed the Instruments: Analyze trades, review data, and identify what worked and what didn't. Don't ignore the whispers of your technical indicators or the echoes of fundamental analysis. Learn from each voyage, both smooth and stormy.
- Trim the Sails: If your plan consistently leads you into choppy waters, consider a more seaworthy design. Don't cling to a sinking ship – be brave enough to rebuild with newfound knowledge and experience.

Remember:

- Consistency is Key: Stick to your plan like a barnacle to a rock (except when the rock crumbles, then adjust!). Discipline is your windward, guiding you through even the fiercest storms.
- Celebrate Milestones: Don't wait for the final treasure chest to crack open. Every successful trade, every conquered fear, every lesson learned – these are victories to be savored.

- Learn and Adapt: The market is a perpetual school, offering endless lessons. Embrace the constant learning curve, and your plan will evolve alongside your trading prowess.